Abiding in Christ
30-day Devotional

"Without me you can do Nothing" (John 15:5).

Nanncie Constantin

Forever Love Jesus—Elm City, NC
ISBN: 979-8-9874971-0-4
eBook ISBN: 979-8-9874971-1-1
Library of Congress Control Number: 2023900912
Title: *Abiding in Christ: 30-day Devotional*
Author: Nanncie Constantin
Digital distribution | 2023
Paperback | 2023

Dedication

To my Lord and Savior Jesus, I wouldn't be where I am today spiritually, physically, emotionally, and financially without His grace and mercy.

To my godly father Louis Constantin and my late mother Ermise Constantin, who has been my example of how man hath to always pray. Thank you for praying for me and all of my siblings. We love you.

To my wonderful husband, my blessing from God, who daily prays and regularly fasts with me. The Bible tells us in the book of Ecclesiastes 4:9, "Two are better than one, because they have good return to their labor." God bless me with a partner with whom we can labor together in prayer before our heavenly Father. He is a true blessing from God. My love forever.

To my wonderful late grandmother, Arshaloos Bell, I remember as a teenager, she inscribed the Word of God in my spirit and my mind; she taught me the importance and power of spending quality time in prayer with the Lord. Her weekly Bible studies taught me how to have a personal, one-on-one relationship with my Lord and Savior, Jesus. What a blessing you were to my family and me. Because of your willingness to go to the mission field, you have led so many to Christ and changed so many lives for the kingdom of God, including my family. I will always love you.

To my personal intercessor, prayer partners, my dear little sister Horlune Constantin, my beautiful older sister in Christ MapitsoMolebatsi Rivera, my dearest best friends, Jessica Contreras, Katrina Caturan Boutrus, Johannah Caturan Pornan, Bonnie Kavolis, Tai Sullivan, Tara Peaco, and many others who have blessed me with their prayers over the years. I love you all.

Contents

In Luke chapter 18 Jesus told His disciple a parable showing them that man should always pray and not give up.

Jesus was our example on earth of how important prayer is. The disciple notice He would wake up early each morning and go and pray, they was so intrigue by it they asked Jesus to teach them how to pray. Imagine out of everything they saw Jesus did (raising the dead, healing the sick, feed the hungry, open the eyes of the blind, walk on water, calming a raging sea, etc.) while walking the earth with Him and the only thing they asked him was to teach them how to pray; which tells me there must be something powerful in prayer.

Prayer is your lifeline to your heavenly Father the maker of all things in heavens, on earth, and the sea (Psalm 146:6). He alone possess the road map of your life, and without a daily communication and guidance it is impossible for anyone to reach their full God giving destiny. One of the best ways I can explain this is a comparison to our earthly parents.

Most children have a daily communication with their earthly parents for guidance, wisdom, without that daily connection with their earthly parents it would be really hard to make good decision. The same way if we don't connect with our heavenly father on a regular basis it will be very hard for us to make good decision in our daily situations.

God is ready to meet with us every day, as many times you would like to come to Him. He is never too busy to listen to his children. God gave us a personal invitation in Jeremiah 33:3 "Call to me and I will answer you and show you great and mighty things you do not know."

Acknowledgements

No project in life can be successful without the help and support of those who love us the most. We can accomplish our goals and dreams much more quickly when we have the support and love from those who claim to love us the most.

To the Holy Spirit who daily guides me into all truth, what a gift from the Father. John 14:16-17 "And I will ask the Father, and He will give you another advocate to help you and be with you forever. The spirit of truth." Thank you, my Lord Jesus, for this priceless gift.

I wish to thank my handsome husband, who has supported me from day one of our marriage. His patience, love, kindness, and meekness are a blessing from God. I prayed and fasted for years for a godly husband, and the Lord answered my prayer and gave me my heart's desire. My achievements are yours also, my love.

To my wonderful siblings, my brothers and sisters, my nieces and nephews, thank you for your love and support. I love you all.

Apostle Cassandra Williams from Mount Pleasant Baptist Church- May you always listen to the Holy Spirit. I was able to write this book because of the 21-day transformation fast the Lord led you to. Ten years ago, God helped me break my fear and write this book He had placed in my heart. I love you, my sister in Christ.

Daily Prayer

Lord I lean to you for strength today. Your word remind me without you I can do nothing, so father please lead and guide me to a closer relationship with you.

Abiding Day 1

John 15:5
"Without me you can do Nothing."

As a young girl, one of my many fears was being outside God's will for my life. I know God sent me here on earth for a specific purpose, but growing up, I didn't always know what that purpose was. From the age of 13 years old, I felt an urgency to seek after God. Therefore, I set aside one day per week to pray to the Lord to ask for wisdom, guidance, and direction for my life. For whatever reason, I chose Monday night from 7 p.m. to 9 p.m. I would read several chapters in the book of Psalms, a chapter in the book of Proverbs, listen to several worship songs, and pray; this was my weekly routine throughout high school.

I was never a rebellious kid growing up. However, once I devoted that one day per week to the Lord, I noticed some positive changes in my daily habits. I was more focused, loving, patient, and kind. I was more sensitive to what I said and did. I can see the Lord's favor and blessing over my life as I continue to seek Him. I was thriving in school, had good health, and had wonderful friends. I felt **the** need **to seek God even more with such a positive outcome**.

At the age of 15 years old, I prayed and asked the Lord to provide me with my first job. Most of my high school friends were working at the mall, making minimum wages of about $5 back then, so I prayed a sample prayer. I remember it like it was yesterday; I asked my heavenly Father to provide me with a higher-paying job so I could save enough money for college. To my expectation, God granted my request; I got my first job at the age of 15, making $9.50 per hour, bringing home close to $1000 per paycheck, which was a lot of money for a teenager back then. I learned at a young age that I could not do anything without God's help.

Daily Reflection: Write down three incidents when God answered a prayer request in your life that exceeded your expectations.

1. _____
2. _____
3. _____

Meditate on this verse throughout the day.

"Without me you can do Nothing." (John 15:5).

Daily Prayer

Father help me to be fruitful and multiple in every area of my life. Help me to accomplish great things for your kingdom. Father help me to stay focus on my appointed kingdom assignment. In Jesus name Amen.

Abiding Day 2

John 15:4
"Abide in Me, and I in you. As the branch cannot
bear fruit of itself unless it abides in the vine, so
neither can you unless you abide in Me."

Webster's definition of the word "Abiding"
is to remain stable or fixed in a state; my
absolute favorite is "continuing for a long
time." Let us take some time to meditate on this verse
and try to apply it to our daily lives or activities. At
the beginning of the verse, we see that the Lord asked
for us to abide in Him, and as a result, He will also
abide in us. The second part of the verse tells us what
will happen if we do not abide in our source of life,
which is Jesus. We will not bear fruit.

The example the Lord gave us from this verse was
a vine three. The branch cannot bear fruit unless it is
attached to the tree. In the same way, with us, we will
never reach our full potential if we are not stable or
fixed in our daily walk with Jesus.

"I am the true vine, and my father is the gardener.
He cuts off every branch in me that bears no fruit,
while every branch that does bear fruit, He prunes so
that it will be even more fruitful" (John 15:1-2).

If you ever have a chance to talk to a farmer, one of
the most important qualities they seek before

4

purchasing a farm is good quality soil. That decision is because a farmer knows good soil is the most essential element since it determines not only what can be grown but whether yields will be high or low. Fruitfulness is a top priority for any farmer.

What should a follower of Jesus get from John 15:1-2? Jesus expects us to be fruitful and multiple in every area of our lives. We each have 24 hours in a day to accomplish great things. We were sent here to earth on an assignment. It is up to us to abide in Jesus to find out what that assignment is.

One of the most important ways to stay abiding in God is through daily prayer and meditation.

List four things you will start doing to stay connected with the Lord on a daily basis.

1. _____

2. _____

3. _____

4. _____

Meditate on this verse today.

"Abide in Me, and I in you. As the branch cannot bear fruit of itself unless it abides in the vine, so neither can you unless you abide in Me" (John 15:4).

Daily Prayer

Father help me to learn how to turn off the lies from this world so I can focus on the mission you have for me.

Abiding Day 3.

John 8:31
"If you continue in My word, then you are truly
disciples of Mine."

I thought the 90s were horrible. Fast forward to
2022. I never thought I would see so much pain
and suffering in the world. I have to say
the pandemic did not make things any easier. I
know 2020 was not easy for most people, but for me,
I have to say it was one of the hardest years of my
life, aside from 2010 when I lost my older sister
due to lung cancer and suffered a major earthquake
in Haiti, the country I was born in.

Friends, if you are truly God's disciples, you
cannot turn a blind eye to all the pain and suffering in
our world today. The number of crimes, famine,
pestilence, plague, earthquakes, wildfires, killings,
godlessness, and lack of impiety, just among a few
things we have to endure in our world, is unthinkable.

I try to stay current with the news daily. However,
when the 2020 pandemic hit our world, I found
myself getting more hopeless because of the amount
of negativity that was pouring out from the media. I
was so sad I couldn't even see the world making it
through the year 2020. May I remind you that I was
praying, reading the Word, yet feeling hopeless

because of the negativity I heard from the news network.

I decided to shut down all the lies from the world and start listening only to the voice of truth. I cut out the lies from the news and stay away from negative people. I meditate on Romans 3:4 daily.

"God forbid: yea, let God be true, but every man a liar" (Romans 3:4).

As I meditate on this truth from the book of Romans, I find myself more encouraged, hopeful, and looking forward to our Lord intervening and rescuing His people from this pandemic. My work as a healthcare provider has more meaning, and my conversations have more meaning. My purpose and vision did not perish because I stayed in the Word of the Lord. I have more determination to continue the race the Lord set before me until the day of my Lord and Savior, Jesus Christ.

"I Press toward the mark for the prize to the high calling of God in Christ Jesus" (Philippians 3:14).

Write down four things God call you to do in this world, and make a promise to God to continue them until He returns.

1. _____
2. _____
3. _____
4. _____

Meditate on this verse today.

"If you continue in My word, then you are truly disciples of Mine" (John 8:31).

Daily Prayer

Holy Spirit give me wisdom to listen to your instruction daily. Let me never ignore any feeling to get closer to you. Father let your will be done in my life always.

Abiding Day 4

2 John 1:9
"Anyone who goes too far and does not abide in the teaching of Christ, does not have God; the one who abides in the teaching, he has both the Father and the Son."

Remember how God granted my prayer request at the age of 15 with a good-paying job to have enough money to go to college? Well, I didn't let God down; I kept my promise to the Lord. I started my freshman year in August 1998 at Bob Jones University as a premed major. You see, my dream at the age of 13 was to be a physician and travel to various countries, including Haiti, to help those less fortunate who cannot afford healthcare.

The first years of college were challenging; at the age of 18 years old, I found myself needing God more than ever. So I decided to increase my once-a-week devotional time with the Lord to three times a week. Again, for whatever reason, in my little 18-year-old mind, I felt the need to seek God more than once a week because my issues were more than when I was 13 years old.

I now know that the feeling I had to draw closer to God was the Holy Spirit, whom Jesus promised us before He ascended to Heaven.

"And I will ask the father, and He will give you another advocate to help you and be with you forever. The spirit of truth..." (John 14:16-17).

Don't ever ignore any urge to get closer to God. The closer to God you are, the more wisdom and understanding you will receive.

Write down four things you will start doing daily to get closer to the Holy Spirit.

1. _____

2. _____

3. _____

4. _____

Meditate on this verse today.

"Anyone who goes too far and does not abide in the teaching of Christ, does not have God; the one who abides in the teaching, he has both the Father and the Son" (2 John 1:9).

Daily Prayer

Father I confess my sins to you today, I know that I am a sinner and that I cannot save myself. Jesus I believe you are the son of God who died on the cross for my sins and rose from the dead on the third day. Thank you for bearing my sins and giving me the gift of eternal life. Please Lord come into my life I made you my Lord and savior today. In Jesus name (Friend if you prayed this prayer by faith you are part of God's family)

Abiding Day 5

Colossians 2:6
"Therefore as you have received Christ Jesus the
Lord, so walk in Him."

I would pray that you have received Jesus as your personal Lord and Savior if you are reading this book. However, if you haven't made that decision or don't know how to take that step, well, you are in luck because I once was in your place.

Even though I grew up in a Christian home, it was not until the age of 13 that I personally decided to make the decision to ask Jesus to be my Lord and Savior. And, friend, I've never regretted that choice.

This verse from below changed my life forever. Knowing that God loves me this much makes me want to know and love Him back.

John 3:16 "For God so Loved the world that He gave His one and only son, that whoever believes in him shall not perish but have eternal life."

I pray that you make this personal and receive this precious gift today.

You see, the world is designed in such a way to make you believe you can make it on your own. All you need is to get more money, fame, wealth, houses, cars, and higher status. Then you will be happy, which in reality is a lie. Don't misunderstand me;

there is nothing wrong with someone working hard to better himself or herself. The problem comes when a person removes God from the picture and tries to make it on his or her own merit.

Remember this verse in the book of John?

"Without me you can do Nothing." (John 15:5).

Look around you; the richest people in the world, who we think have it all, are the most depressed and loneliest. Most of them end their lives because of what they thought would satisfy them.

I am a firm believer that God has a purpose and plan for everyone. And that purpose and plan is to prosper us, but we can't do it without God's guidance.

"I know the plans I have for you declares the Lord, The plans to prosper you and not to harm you, plan to give you hope and a future" (Jeremiah 29:11).

Write down four things you will practice daily to walk in God's plan for you.

1. _____
2. _____
3. _____
4. _____

Meditate on this verse today.

"Therefore as you have received Christ Jesus the Lord, so walk in Him" (Colossians 2:6).

Daily Prayer

Father Help me to learn how to set my mind on things above, may I cherish your word daily so I can get more wisdom and understanding on how to live a Christ center life. In Jesus name. Amen.

Abiding Day 6

Colossians 3:1
"Therefore if you have been raised up with Christ,
keep seeking the things above, where Christ is, seated
at the right hand of God."

L et's face it; the world has a way of getting us
down. The year 2020 alone is enough to get
anyone down. Perhaps you have felt
overwhelmed by the corruption and confusion that is
going on worldwide. If we don't keep seeking
wisdom from above, even the day-to-day tasks that
we are given, whether for our career, taking care of
our family, or loving our neighbors as ourselves, can
feel burdensome.

The Bible gives us a clear guideline on how to stay
focused on heavenly things. Through the power of the
Holy Spirit, we can overcome any worldly temptation.

"Put to death, therefore whatever belongs to your
earthly nature. Sexual immorality, impurity, lust, evil
desires and greed, which is idolatry."
(Colossians 3:5).

It is very hard to achieve a heavenly mindset while
pursuing the things of this world. When we focus on
earthly things, our heavenly purpose will get left
behind. Turn your gaze away from the things of this

16

world and instead place your peace and eternal faith in our Lord and Savior, Jesus Christ.

One of the best ways I keep my heart and mind on things above is by cherishing God's Word daily. One cannot expect a Christ-centered life by consuming the things of this world. The world feeds on fear, greed, unfairness, manipulation, backstabbing, and lies. The Bible is a road map for our journey through this life. Reading it will make us grow closer to our Lord, who is seated at the right hand of God and forever interceding for us.

Write down four daily practices you will use to seek the things above.

1. _____

2. _____

3. _____

4. _____

"Therefore if you have been raised up with Christ, keep seeking the things above, where Christ is, seated at the right hand of God" (Colossians 3:1).

Daily Prayer

Heavenly father help me to learn how to put to death whatever belong to my earthly nature, help me to get rid of every lustful desires, greed, and impure thoughts in Jesus name.

Abiding Day 7

Colossians 3:3
"Set your mind on the things above, not on the things that are on earth. For you have died and your life is hidden with Christ in God."

Chapter 3 of the book of Colossians really focuses on how to set our eyes on things above. We will focus on several things we can do as Christians to help accomplish that task.

1. Put to death earthly things. Get rid of your old habits.

"Put to death, therefore whatever belongs to your earthly nature. Sexual immorality, impurity, lust, evil desires and greed, which is idolatry" (Colossians 3:5).

"Therefore if any man be in Christ, he is a new creature, old things are passed away, behold all things are become new" (2 Corinthians 5:17).

2. Put on the new self which you received through Christ Jesus.
"Where there is neither Greek nor Jew, circumcision nor uncircumcision, barbarian, Scythian, bond nor free: but Christ is all, and in all" (Colossians 3:11).

Through the empowering of His Holy Spirit and the transformation of our minds as we read and meditate on His Word, God has given us the ability to reject sin and temptation.

2 Peter 1:3 says, "According as his divine power hath given unto us all things that pertain unto life and godliness, through the knowledge of Him that hath called us to glory and virtue."

Another way to stay focused on the things above is to embrace the new self through the power of the Holy Spirit.

3.   Find peace through Christ

"Let the peace of Christ rule in your heart, since as members of one body you were called to peace" (Colossians 3:15.

All the things going on in our world right now can easily take our peace of mind. Forget the eternal promise we have in Christ Jesus. Our minds are so powerful that we need to be careful about what we think and what we allow to enter our minds. The book of Proverbs says it nicely.

Proverb 23:7 says, "For as a man thinks in his heart, so is he."

So choose to think positively, have uplifting conversations, and increase your faith instead of your fear.

"Thou will keep him in perfect peace, whose mind is stayed on thee, because he trust in thee" (Isaiah 26:3.

4.   Be thankful in all you do.

"And whatsoever ye do in word or deed, do all in the name of the Lord Jesus, giving thanks to God and the father by Him" (Colossians 3:17).

Thankfulness may not come easily, but as believers, we must remind ourselves that being thankful in every situation is one of the best weapons we can use against the enemy. Being thankful shifts our focus from our worries to God's awesome power to provide. So let us stay focused on the things above by being thankful in all situations.

Write down four things you will put to death, one after another, to get closer to God.

1. _____
2. _____
3. _____
4. _____

Meditate on this verse today.

"Set your mind on the things above, not on the things that are on earth. For you have died and your life is hidden with Christ in God" (Colossians 3:3).

Daily Prayer

Father may I faithfully serve you until I finish my race here on earth, may I hear well done my serve when I see you face to face.

Abiding Day 8

1 John 2:28
"Now, little children, abide in Him, so that when He appears, we may have confidence and not shrink away from Him in shame at His coming."

When I first read this verse, two words stood out to me: "shrink and shame." So I asked the Holy Spirit to help me gain more confidence so I would not shrink away in shame at the Lord's coming. Being in shame before our Lord is something every believer needs to avoid, and we should strive for the positive result of being confident before our Lord.

Friends, it is possible to be a believer in Christ and yet not abide in Him. At the beginning of this book, I told you guys that the year 2020 was one of the hardest years of my life because I had never experienced a pandemic in my lifetime as horrible as COVID-19. I was so focused on the news and the outcome of the pandemic that I totally neglected my personal devotional and prayer times with the Lord.

I find myself operating in fear instead of faith. I was afraid to go to work because I didn't want to get the virus and die prematurely. It wasn't until I shot down the negative news and started reading the

Word, praying, and fasting that my faith began to increase.

"Be strong and of good courage, fear not, nor be afraid of them; for the Lord thy God, he it is that doth go with thee; He will not fail thee, nor forsake thee."
(Deuteronomy 31:6).

I meditated on that Word day and night. I started to encourage myself in the Lord, and soon after, all fear, worries, and disbelief completely left my mind.

So I made the decision to abide in Christ by studying His Word and believing His promises, and as a result, I received His peace, joy, and happiness.

Write down four things you will apply from God's Word to increase your confidence in Christ.

1. _____

2. _____

3. _____

4. _____

Meditate on this verse today.

"Now, little children, abide in Him, so that when He appears, we may have confidence and not shrink away from Him in shame at His coming"
(1 John 2:28).

Daily Prayer

Father give me a heart to love and obey you daily. Help me to set a watch over my mouth so I don't say or do anything that would offend anyone. Help me to love people as you love them. In Jesus name. Amen.

Abiding Day 9

John 15:10
"If you keep My commandments, you will abide in
My love; just as I have kept My Father's
commandments and abide in His love."

This verse is plain and simple. If any Christian ever wonders what the one way he or she can abide in the Lord is, look no further. While doing Jesus' ministry on earth, He told his disciples one of the best ways to abide in His love was to keep His commandments. The disciples had a question most people still ask even today.

"Which is the greatest commandment in the Law?"

Jesus answered them by saying this in the book of Matthew 22:37-40.

"Jesus replied, 'Love the Lord your God with all your heart and with all our soul and with all your mind. This is the first and greatest commandment. And the second is like it; love your neighbors as yourself. All the law and the prophets hang on these two commandments.'"

Easy enough, right? Well, it is sad that many Christians today have difficulty obeying these two sample commandments. So many churches today focus on pleasing people instead of God. Many preachers are so afraid of offending people that they refuse to rebuke sins in the church. Many churches across America remove prayer meetings and Bible studies from the church for the convenience of the church members.

Romans 10:17 "So then faith comes by hearing, and hearing by the word of God."

How are we supposed to grow and abide in Christ if churches are removing Bible study and Sunday school?

"Hear the word of the Lord, because the Lord has a charge to bring against you who live in the land. There is no faithfulness, no love, no acknowledgment of God in the land. There is only cursing, lying, and murder, stealing, and adultery. Because of this the land dries up and all who live in it waste away." (Hosea 4:1-3).

It is frightening to read this verse. However, everything the prophet Hosea mentions in this verse is true in our society today. Each of those actions is a violation of God's commandments. How can we love God or our neighbors if we continually curse, lie, steal, and kill one another? If we want to transform our lives and truly abide in Christ, we need to know God's character and requirements and live in obedience to those requirements.

Write down four attributes of God that would help you keep His commandments.

1. _____
2. _____
3. _____
4. _____

Meditate on this verse today.

"If you keep My commandments, you will abide in My love; just as I have kept My Father's commandments and abide in His love" (John 15:10).

Daily Prayer

Father give me daily wisdom to practice the fruit of the Spirit, may love, joy, peace, kindness, self-control be second nature to me. In Jesus name. Amen.

Abiding Day 10

Galatians 5:22-23
"But the fruit of the Spirit is love, joy, peace, patience, kindness, goodness, faithfulness, gentleness, self-control; against such things there is no law."

How must we practice the fruit of the Spirit daily to get closer to God? Let's take some time and break each down into a clearer understanding.

Love

"Love never fails" (1 Corinthians 13).

Love is a decision one must choose to make daily. It takes effort and wiliness to love. That is true in every relationship, including marriage, family, neighbors, and coworkers. Ask the Holy Spirit daily to help you learn how to practice love in your daily encounters.

Joy

Most people experience joy when something positive happens in their love life. Maybe they get a raise, get married, or get a new job. But have you ever been around someone filled with joy just because he or she has the Lord? Such a person is contagious. Always up-lifting. They can light up a room just by walking into it. One thing that gives me joy on a daily basis is the hope that I get to spend eternity with my Creator at the end of this life. Salvation is my primary reason for having joy in this life.

"For the joy of the Lord is your strength" (Nehemiah 8:10).

Peace

"Peace I leave with you, my peace I give you, I do not give to you as the world gives. Do not let your hearts be troubled and do not be afraid" (John 14: 27).

To have peace is to believe that God is in control and has a plan for your life. When we let our hearts be troubled by the problems of this life, we tend to make bad decisions and react prematurely. A peaceful person is more rounded, fearless, and open to hearing God's instructions.

Patience

"Be patient, then brother, until the Lord's coming" (James 5:7).

We are a generation of "I want it now"; we want everything right now. We expect fast food and high-speed internet; the second we don't get it our way, we get upset, disappointed, and complain. One of the things I've learned working in the healthcare system is patience. Most of my patients feel more appreciated and cared for when a provider gives them their attention and time. Patients would tell me they prefer one provider over the next simply because of good bedside manners. One provider was more patient than the other.

Kindness

Showing kindness to someone is one of the most satisfying things a person can do. There should not be any exception to when we show kindness to others. A small act, like letting someone get in front of you at the grocery store checkout line, can brighten someone's day. You never know how your kindness can bring blessings into someone's life.

"Do not forget to show hospitality to strangers, for by so doing some people have shown hospitality to angels without knowing it" (Hebrew 13:2).

Goodness

"You are good, and do good; teach me your statutes" (Psalm 119:68).

Goodness is holding firm to what is right, no matter the circumstances. Hold true to your integrity. So many people allow their situation to dictate how they will behave. Your character says a lot about the action you will take in a stressful situation. Always pick goodness over wickedness.

Faithfulness

We don't always have all of the answers to why certain things happen in our lives. But one thing is certain: as Christians, we know that God loves us and that He promises to work everything out in our favor. Commit to seeking God daily and remaining faithful in all that you do, and the blessing will come.

"The Lord will perfect that which concerns me" (Psalm 138:8).

Gentleness

One of my favorite verses about gentleness is found in 1 Peter 3:4 "Rather, it should be that of your inner self, the unfading beauty of a gentle and quiet spirit, which is of great worth in God's sight."

Approach a situation with concern. Gentleness and truth are the best ways a person can resolve any conflict. Do not belittle people with your words or actions. Do or say to others what you would like them to do or say to you.

Self-control

"A man without self-control is like a city broken into and left without walls" (Proverbs 25:28).

Nowadays, people have no self-control. They make impulsive decisions or say hurtful things to people they love and later regret them. Self-control takes practice and discipline. Without God, it is impossible for people to stay consistent with self-control.

Self-control was one of the fruit of the Spirit I prayed for daily because I know once you put your words or actions on the table, it is very hard to take them back.

Make a commitment by choosing four fruit of the Spirit that you will practice on a daily basis.

1. _____
2. _____
3. _____
4. _____

Meditate on the verse throughout the day.

"But the fruit of the Spirit is love, joy, peace, patience, kindness, goodness, faithfulness, gentleness, self-control; **against such things there is no law**" (Galatians 5:22-23).

Daily Prayer

Father thank you for a personal invitation to come boldly before your throne. I know you always have my best interest at heart, may I never forget how bless I am to be part of your kingdom.

Abiding Day 11

John 15:7
"If you abide in Me, and My words abide in you, ask whatever you wish, and it will be done for you."

This verse gives us a personal invitation from the Lord Himself to abide in Him. Just imagine the blessing and peace that comes when we truly abide in the Lord. Jesus saved the whole world because He abided in the Father.

Because of His constant connection with the Father, He never turned away from His missions; even when Satan attempted to turn Jesus away from His mission several times, He never did. This could be true for us. We were sent on earth to accomplish a specific purpose. If we are not abiding in the Lord, we will never fulfill our destiny.

Below are some verses that talk about abiding in Jesus:

"Abide in me, and I in you. As the branch cannot bear fruit by itself, unless it abides in the vine, neither can you, unless you abide in me" (John 15:4).

How does a person abide in Christ? First, you must be born again. Make a decision to let Jesus be your Lord and Savior. Once that decision is made, start reading and obeying His Word. Too often, people will decide to follow Jesus but never truly commit to Him. To be productive in this Christian journey, you must stay connected to the Lord.

"Whoever keeps his commandments abides in God, and God in him. And by this we know that he abides in us, by the Spirit whom he has given us" (1 John 3:4).

Have you ever heard the phrase "you can tell a person by their fruit?" Many people will die and never experience a blessing they couldn't have had while on earth.

"Therefore, as you received Christ Jesus the Lord, so walk in him" (Colossians 2:6).

Write down four things you will start doing to abide in the Lord starting today.

1. _____

2. _____

3. _____

4 _____

Meditate on the verse throughout the day.

"If you abide in Me, and My words abide in you, ask whatever you wish, and it will be done for you"
(John 15:7).

Daily Prayer

Father help me to stay focus on my mission, help me to walk in the same manner as Christ did, remove every distraction far from me, give me discipline so I can accomplish the task you have for my life.

Abiding Day 12

1 John 2:6
"The one who says he abides in Him ought himself to walk in the same manner as He walked."

Jesus had a finite amount of time on earth to complete His mission; 33 years to be exact. So He had no time to waste. He stayed focused on the mission, even when His own mother and brother tried to disrupt Him; He had to remind them that He was about His Father's business. It is not impossible for a person to walk in the same manner as Christ because the Lord promises in John 14:12, "He that believes on me, the works that I do shall he do also, and greater works than these shall he do."

To walk in the same manner as Christ, a person must avoid distraction, stay focused, and stay in the Word. Our time on earth is very short; there is no need to waste it. Prayer was one of the greatest examples of what Jesus did to stay abiding with the Father. Jesus' disciples were so intrigued by the amount of time Jesus placed on prayer that they made sure to ask the Lord to teach them how to pray.

"Now Jesus was praying in a certain place, and when He finished, one of his disciples said to him Lord, teach us to pray" (Luke 11:1). Despite everything they saw the Lord do, prayer was the only thing they wanted to learn.

What triggered the disciples' curiosity to ask the Lord to teach them how to pray?

I believe the number one reason they asked the Lord to teach them how to pray was so that they could see the power, the connection, and anointing Jesus had over His life. Nothing was out of reach for the Lord. Through daily prayer, Jesus sought direction from the Father for His ministry on earth. Prayer was a priority for the Lord; the disciples experienced miracles after miracles, and the one thing they noticed the Lord doing the most was prayer. So clearly, praying is one of the key ways to get things done in this world.

There was one of the stories in the Gospel of Matthew where the disciples experienced some pushback when they tried to cast out a demon from a young boy; they didn't have the power to cast out the demon. They had to wait for Jesus to return and cast the demons out. Afterward, the disciple asks the Lord why they couldn't cast out the demon. He told them something interesting. "However, this kind does not go out except by prayer and fasting" (Matthew 17:21). So it's not that they couldn't cast the demons out, but they weren't prepared. That tells me that if the disciples had been praying and fasting on a daily basis like Jesus, they could have easily cast out that demon.

"Verily, verily I say unto you, He that believeth on me, the works that I do shall he do also; and greater works than these shall he do; because I go unto my father" (John 14:12).

If I can encourage any believer to stay abiding in Christ and accomplish their mission in this world, it is to make prayer and fasting a priority.

Make a vow to God that you will spend 20-30 minutes per day praying and fasting as often as possible.

Write down four ways you will apply discipline in your life to make prayer a priority.

1. _____
2. _____
3. _____
4. _____

Meditate on the verse throughout the day/

"The one who says he abides in Him ought himself to walk in the same manner as He walked" (1 John 2:6).

Daily Prayer

Father help me to stay committed to the calling you
have over my life.

Abiding Day 13

Revelation 3:20
"Behold, I stand at the door and knock; if anyone
hears My voice and opens the door, I will come in to
him and will dine with him, and he with Me."

This verse pictures Jesus standing outside,
knocking, patiently waiting to be invited into
our hearts. So Jesus is looking for any
invitation from any responsive individual who is truly
ready to make a commitment. If you can hear the
knock and open the door of your heart, He promises
to dine with you.

Have you ever wondered why the Lord doesn't just
force His way into our hearts? Why does the Lord
choose to wait for our response?

This invitation is so sacred that Jesus would be out
of character if He forced himself on us. We must
want this intimacy with Him. Love cannot be forced.
A husband cannot force love on his wife; neither can
a wife force love on her husband; the relationship
won't last.

People who feel pushed or threatened to do
anything against their will can easily tell that they feel
violated. I think that is one of the reasons the Lord
chose to wait for us to open the doors of our hearts to
Him instead of forcefully taking them. Your

permission is very important to the Lord. The day you choose to open that door tells the Lord you are ready and committed to having a relationship with Him.

You have a choice. You can either open the door of your heart today and let Jesus in and experience the unfathomable transformation or keep the door of your heart closed and never experience the life you were meant to live.

Jesus wants to transform your life, but you must be willing and ready to take that journey. He will not force anything on you, so don't delay. We all have an expiration date because we don't know the date, the time, or the hour. I would advise you to open the door of your heart sooner rather than later.

The choice is yours. Choose now.

Write down four things you will place in your heart to help keep the door of your heart open to the Lord.

1. _____

2. _____

3. _____

4. _____

Meditate on the verse today.

"Behold, I stand at the door and knock; if anyone hears My voice and opens the door, I will come in to him and will dine with him, and he with Me" (Revelation 3:20).

Daily Prayer

Holy Spirit open my eye to the things of God; help me daily to live a Godly life.

Abiding Day 14

Romans 8:9-10

"However, you are not in the flesh but in the Spirit, if indeed the Spirit of God dwells in you. But if anyone does not have the Spirit of Christ, he does not belong to Him. If Christ is in you, though the body is dead because of sin, yet the spirit is alive because of righteousness."

Once you decide to open your heart to Jesus and make Him your Lord and Savior, you receive a special gift, God's Holy Spirit. Therefore, you no longer live in the flesh but in the Spirit. Daily, you should strive to live a godly lifestyle by rejecting sin and pressing for holiness.

"Therefore if anyone is in Christ, he is a new creation, old things have passed away; behold all things have become new" (2 Corinthians 5:17).

The Spirit of God's primary job is to guide us into all truth. We live in a dark world where the devil is at the centre of everything. What used to be wrong now is right, and what used to be right now is considered wrong. If we are not abiding in the Word, we can start letting this world's lies and false teachings get into our daily lives. As a result, we can begin acting and doing things in the flesh.

"But when He, the Spirit of truth comes, He will guide you into all truth" (John 16:13).

Instead of listening to social media and news networks, stay current by reading the Bible. Ask the Holy Spirit to guide you in the knowledge and truth of God's Word.

I'm not against social media and technology. I think it is one of the tools Christians can use to further God's kingdom in this world. What I'm against is when I see Christians failing to represent the Lord on these platforms.

Many Christian priorities, including top preachers from mega-churches worldwide, are shifting away from God. Our visions and desires are no longer about the kingdom of God, but more so about the things of this world. When I see thousands of Facebook pages and YouTube channels focusing on worldly things such as fame, how to get rich quick, how to build the next million-dollar empire, and very few topics on how to get eternal life and how to save your soul from eternal damnation, it makes me think Christians are living more in the flesh than the spirit.

Christians are not experiencing the full power of the Holy Spirit because we are not abiding in Christ but rather focusing on materialistic things that we cannot take with us to Heaven.

Write down four obstacles in your life that prevent you from living by the Spirit.

1. _____

2. _____

3. _____

4. _____

Now write down ways you are planning to overcome these four things through the Holy Spirit.

1. _____
2. _____
3. _____
4 _____

Meditate on this verse today.

"However, you are not in the flesh but in the Spirit, if indeed the Spirit of God dwells in you. But if anyone does not have the Spirit of Christ, he does not belong to Him. If Christ is in you, though the body is dead because of sin, yet the spirit is alive because of righteousness" (Romans 8:9-10).

Daily Prayer

Lord when things are hard, help me to learn how to
run to you for help instead of running to the world.

Abiding Day 15

Ephesians 3:17-19
"So that Christ may dwell in your hearts through faith; and that you, being rooted and grounded in love, may be able to comprehend with all the saints what is the breadth and length and height and depth, and to know the love of Christ which surpasses knowledge, that you may be filled up to all the fullness of God."

Once you open your heart to the Lord and completely surrender your will, then you will start to experience the true love of Christ. To make Christ at home in your home, you need to stay anchored in His Word through prayer and fasting. See, prayer is the way a Christian can access Heaven. It's the way we bring God's purpose and vision into this world.

We have countless examples in the Bible where godly men and women prayed and fasted to see God's will accomplished in the world. A prime example was Queen Esther, when she declared a fast for three days. As a result of this, the entire Jewish nation was saved. Daniel and Nehemiah turned to prayer, and as a result, God promised to restore the Jewish nation to the promise land.

"And if Children, also heirs: Heirs of God, and joint-heirs with Christ; if so be that we suffer with him, that we may be also glorified together" (Romans 8:17).

So when we pray, we should come boldly to the throne because we belong to this great family; because of Jesus' sacrifice on the Cross, we have the privilege of coming before the Father with our requests through prayers.

Write down four ways you will open your heart to gain more knowledge about Christ.

1. _____

2. _____

3. _____

4. _____

Meditate on this verse today.

"So that Christ may dwell in your hearts through faith; and that you, being rooted and grounded in love, may be able to comprehend with all the saints what is the breadth and length and height and depth, and to know the love of Christ which surpasses knowledge, that you may be filled up to all the fullness of God" (Ephesians 3:17-19).

Daily Prayer

Lord may I never stray away from your truth because of hardship instead let your word of truth lead me to everlasting peace.

Abiding Day 16

1 John 2:24

"As for you, let that abide in you which you heard from the beginning. If what you heard from the beginning abides in you, you also will abide in the Son and in the Father."

L et the Word and the truth of God you've learned from the beginning abide in you. So often, I hear Christian testimonies about how they had fallen away from the faith due to problems and circumstances in their lives but were able to return to the faith because of something they learned or heard at the beginning of their lives.

"Train up a child in the way he should go; and when he is old, he will not depart from it" (Proverb 22:6).

I think abiding in the Lord starts in childhood. As parents, we must make it a priority to train our children in the ways of the Lord. Every parent will have to train their children in some way, shape, or form. We have parents who are very disciplinarian and we have parents who are very laid back.

As a Christian parent, you must pray for wisdom when raising your children. Your main goal must be to raise your children to love the Lord and make every effort to obey His Word.

God made you a parent for a reason. God implanted the heavenly wisdom and understanding you need to raise your children in the right way. Always let your children know that what God thinks of them is far more important than man, because they will only answer to God at the end of this life.

God made it abundantly clear to the children of Israel how they should raise their children, teaching them His status and commandments.

"You shall teach them diligently to your children and shall talk of them when you sit in your house and when you walk by the way, and when you lie down, and when you rise up" (Deuteronomy 6:7).

My earthly father engraved this principle into myself and my siblings from a young age. My father was not always physically with us. When I turned 14, my father left and stayed in Haiti full-time as a missionary, while we stayed in Maryland for school. One thing I remember from my father is that he would always tell us that God sees everything we do, good or bad, and one day we will have to answer to God for our actions. He always encourages us to make godly decisions, even in his absence.

A lot of the good decisions I made as a teenager and as an adult were because my earthly father trained me in the way of the Lord.

Discussing God with your children is one way to ensure that they continue to abide in Him. This world is trying to remove Jesus from everything. If parents don't prioritize talking about God with their children, the devil will use the world to talk them into the kingdom of darkness.

I heard a saying a long time ago, "If the devil can talk mighty angels out of Heaven, he can talk men into Hell."

Fill your mind with the Word of God by reading it, meditating on it, and talking about it often so that you can engrave it into your spirit, so when the enemy comes out with his lies, you can use the Word of God against him.

Write out four things you will start implementing in your daily activities to make God a priority.

1. _____

2. _____

3. _____

4. _____

Meditate on this verse today.

"As for you, let that abide in you which you heard from the beginning. If what you heard from the beginning abides in you, you also will abide in the Son and in the Father" (1 John 2:24).

Daily Prayer

Heavenly father help me to represent you well in this world may I never mistreat anyone. May your light within me shine bright so others may glorify you as a result. In Jesus name. Amen

Abiding Day 17

1 John 3:24
"The one who keeps His commandments abides in
Him, and He in him. We know by this that He abides
in us, by the Spirit whom He has given us."

If you do what is right before the Lord by obeying
His commandments, then you can be certain you
are abiding in Christ.

Have you ever heard the expression, "You can tell a
person by their fruit?" These are all accurate statements.

You cannot go around telling people what a good
Christian you are and mistreating others. Your words
have to equal your actions.

During my college years in Greenville, SC, I
worked as a waitress at a well-known restaurant.
Sunday lunch was one of the worst times for
waitresses at that restaurant. One of the reasons was
the treatment of the waitresses by so-called Christians
who came out to eat with their families after church.
They would scream, always want their food to be
discounted for some reason, never be satisfied with
the service they received, and sadly, they are the
worst tippers. Most, if not all, of the waitresses would
be very reluctant to pick up their tables due to fear of
being mistreated and not getting adequate tips for
their labor.

I used to be so ashamed because the non-Christian waitress would tell me if that's the way Christians treat people, they don't ever want to be a Christian. It was so hard to be a testimony for Christ because of past experiences those waitresses had with Christians who would dine at that restaurant after church.

What these so-called Christians didn't realize is that they are Christ's ambassadors and must represent Him well. It's not just dressing up and going to church; minutes after leaving the church, you have road rage because someone cut you in traffic, mistreating waitresses while eating out, or talking down to the janitor or housekeeping who is cleaning your room. You cannot truly abide in Christ while mistreating other people.

As Christians, we must always treat everyone with love and kindness. Remember, we are representatives of Christ and not of ourselves. If you remember from a few chapters back, one fruit of the Spirit was kindness. You never know how you will change someone by just being kind to them.

Write down four things you will put into practice to show more kindness to strangers.

1. _____
2. _____
3. _____
4. _____

Meditate on this verse today.

"The one who keeps His commandments abides in Him, and He in him. We know by this that He abides in us, by the Spirit whom He has given us" (1 John 3:24).

Daily Prayer

Father thank you for the gift of the Holy Spirit, help me to learn how not to grieve the Holy Spirit.

Abiding Day 18

John 14:17
"That is the Spirit of truth, whom the world cannot receive, because it does not see Him or know Him, but you know Him because He abides with you and will be in you."

One of the many blessings Jesus promised His children before leaving this world is the gift of the Holy Spirit. One of the Holy Spirit's jobs is to guide us into God's truth. Understanding who the Holy Spirit is and the important role He plays in our lives is vital to the Christian walk.

When a person makes a personal decision to open their heart to God, it's the Holy Spirit that comes and abides in that person. The Holy Spirit is God's presence in a believer's life on earth.

"But it is written, eye has not seen, nor ear heard, nor has it entered into the heart of man the things which God has prepared for those who love him. But God has revealed them to us by His Spirit for the Spirit searches all things, yes the deep things of God. For what man knows the things of a man except the spirit of man which is in him? Likewise, no one knows the things of God except the Spirit of God" (1 Corinthians 2:9-11).

The Holy Spirit knows the Father. For example, when you are reading a specific verse in the Bible or listening to a sermon and have a strong feeling that the verse or sermon is describing what you are going through, that feeling or sense is the Holy Spirit at work in your life.

Another good example is when the Holy Spirit is working in a new believer's life, all of a sudden, the things of the world that used to be pleasurable before salvation are no longer pleasurable. I have heard stories from many new Christians who would say, "I used to feel no guilt when I used to curse, lie, go clubbing, and have sex outside of marriage, but since I asked Jesus into my life, I have no desire to do those things anymore." Friends, that's the Holy Spirit at work in that individual's life to change them into the image of God.

You see, when a person is in the world without the Spirit of God, he or she doesn't know any truth. It's like living in spiritual darkness with no true knowledge of God. Therefore, the things of this world are true for them. Once he or she makes the decision to be part of the kingdom of God, his or her spiritual eyes are now open by the power of God's Holy Spirit, and now the things of the world are no longer satisfied.

"Likewise the Spirit also helps in our weaknesses. For we do not know what we should pray for as we ought, but the Spirit Himself makes intercession for us with groanings which cannot be uttered." (Romans 8:26).

Now that you know the important role of the Holy Spirit in a believer's daily life, write down four ways you plan to get closer to the Holy Spirit of God.

1. _____

2. _____

3. _____

4. _____

Meditate on this verse today.

"That is the Spirit of truth, whom the world cannot receive, because it does not see Him or know Him, but you know Him because He abides with you and will be in you." (John 14:17).

Daily Prayer

Holy Spirit thank you for teaching me the way of truth, what a blessing to have you guiding me through this life.

Abiding Day 19

1 John 2:27

"As for you, the anointing which you received from
Him abides in you, and you have no need for anyone
to teach you; but as His anointing teaches you about
all things, and is true and is not a lie, and just as it has
taught you, you abide in Him."

As Christians, we have special insight through
the Holy Spirit's guidance. Out of all the many
roles the Holy Spirit plays in a Christian life,
making us more like Christ is one of my favorite and
most important roles. The Holy Spirit equips believers
throughout the Bible to help them fulfill their callings.

There are numerous examples in the Bible of how
God equipped His saints through the Holy Spirit; one
of my favorites comes from Exodus.

In Exodus 31:1-4, it says, "Then the Lord spoke to
Moses, saying: See I have called by name Bezalel the
son of Uri, the son of Hur, of the tribe of Judah. And I
have filled him with the Holy Spirit of God, in
wisdom, in understanding, in knowledge and in all
manner of workmanship, to design artistic works...."

You see, the Lord had a conversation with Moses
about building the tabernacle, a place where He could
dwell with His people. God had specific instructions
on how the tabernacle was supposed to be built, to the

point where He chose certain craftsmanship to further anoint with His Holy Spirit to gain more wisdom and knowledge; God's Holy Spirit was important in that story because, without it, that workmanship would not have the wisdom and knowledge to carry out the work according to God's will.

Friends, the Holy Spirit can operate in the same way in your life today. If you notice chaos in your day-to-day life, your family, your job, or your relationship, stop and take some time to pray and ask the Holy Spirit to give you more wisdom and knowledge on how to fix things in your life. If you are failing at your job, ask God's Holy Spirit for more wisdom. If you fail at parenting, marriage, or friendship, ask God's Holy Spirit to help you.

The Spirit of God is willing and able to do immeasurable more than all we ask or imagine.

Write down four areas in your life where you are failing, and make a promise to seek the Holy Spirit for guidance in those areas daily.

1. _____

2. _____

3. _____

4. _____

Meditate on the verse today.

"As for you, the anointing which you received from Him abides in you, and you have no need for anyone to teach you; but as His anointing teaches you about all things, and is true and is not a lie, and just as it has taught you, you abide in Him" (1 John 2:27).

Daily Prayer

Father thank you for your grace, love and acceptance.

Abiding Day 20

2 Corinthians 5:17
"Therefore if anyone is in Christ, he is a new creature; the old things passed away; behold, new things have come."

This verse reminds me of the Lord's love for us; regardless of where you are in life, Jesus sees you, and all He needs is for you to open the door of your heart and let Him in. While doing Jesus' ministry on earth, He made it a habit to go after what the Pharisees would call sinners.

I am going to share one of my favorite stories in the Bible to help illustrate the love of God. This beautiful story is found in the book of John, the 4th chapter.

The woman at the well.

This story illustrates love, acceptance, and redemption for a woman who people in her own society wouldn't even associate with. It was so bad she would only go to the well when no one else was there to avoid being talked against; see, this woman was what our modern society would call a "home wrecker" she had been with multiple men, and not one of them was her husband. Still, our Lord made a special appointment and knocked at her door. She decided to open and let Him in; her life was never the same.

I always wonder why the Lord never named the Samaritan woman by name. With such a special encounter where this woman's entire life changed, not only did she receive eternal salvation, but the Bible tells us her entire village came to salvation because of her testimony. You would think her name would be mentioned in the Bible. The Holy Spirit revealed to me that her name is unimportant, but her story is. This woman's story can easily be my story, your story, or anyone who feels like an outcast by society. As the Lord took time to meet with this Samaritan woman, so too will He take time to come and meet with you and change your life for the better.

The Bible tells us that after Jesus' encounter with this woman, her entire life was changed. She becomes a new creature, gives up her old lifestyle, and completely devotes her life to Christ. As a result of her encounter with the Lord, many others from our town became believers.

Your testimony has power; you never know how your pain and suffering in this life can change someone else. Your suffering can be used by Jesus to bring someone into His kingdom.

This story is a prime example of Jesus' love and acceptance of sinners. Jesus is ready, standing at the door knocking; choose to be like the Samaritan woman who received Jesus' salvation and changed her life and her entire town.

Write down four bad habits the Lord saved you from or four habits you would like the Lord to take away. Testify with others of the Lord's goodness in your life.

1. _____

2. _____

3. _____

4. _____

Meditate on this verse today.

"Therefore if anyone is in Christ, he is a new creature; the old things passed away; behold, new things have come" (2 Corinthians 5:17).

Daily Prayer

Father may I never let the enemy use shame and guilt as a weapon to draw me away from you, instead remind me of your love and grace that covers multitude of sin.

Abiding Day 21

Romans 8:1
"Therefore there is now no condemnation for those
who are in Christ Jesus."

F eelings of shame, hopelessness, and guilt are
some of the enemy's most common weapons to
keep people down. If you feel condemned, you
are less likely to pray or seek God.

Adam and Eve are our first examples in the Bible
where guilt and shame cause them to hide from the
Lord instead of running to the Lord. Sadly, the enemy
continues to use the same tactic to plague Christians
with guilt and shame to this day.

Often, Christians who feel condemned because of a
sinful lifestyle or a dark past have a hard time finding
joy and hope in the Christian walk; they feel like they
are glued to their sins forever.

But friends, I have good news: we have hope
because Jesus died on the cross to take away our sins,
guilt, and shame. Once you make the decision to open
your heart to Jesus, all of your sins and wrongs are
made right through Him.

Several years ago, I had a conversation with my
older brother about something he went through in his
early twenties. At the age of 19, my brother had his
first baby out of wedlock. It was a very hard time for

him because our father was a pastor, and having a baby out of wedlock was forbidden. Due to fear of my parents, my brother decided to keep the baby a secret. Fast forward five years later, my brother was in seminar school, graduating at the top of his class. However, the secret he held on to for so long was destroying his life. He lives in constant fear, shame, and worry about what men would think of him if they discovered his secret.

My brother told me one day that he was having a conversation with his best friend about it, and his best friend shared Romans 8:1 with him. Afterward, he asked my brother a simple question: Did you confess your sin to the Lord?

My brother replies, "Yes."

Did you receive Jesus' forgiveness?

My brother answered, "Yes."

My brother's friend replied, "You must forgive yourself and move on with the life God has prepared for you."

My brother told me that after reading Romans 8:1, he felt relief, as if he had just dropped a heavy weight he had been carrying for years. After hearing my brother's story, I know the Holy Spirit used my brother's best friend to free him from that condemnation he had been carrying for so long.

See, the day my brother repented, his sins were forgiven; however, he was not able to receive God's forgiveness because of condemnation. So many people are in a similar situation, letting their past situation keep them from moving forward with their destiny. Friend, once you ask for forgiveness, the Bible states your sins are washed away.

I truly believe how a person chooses to respond after sinning says a lot about their walk with God, and once you repent, you need to move on with the rest of your life and sin no more. Time is short; do not let guilt, shame, and condemnation prevent you from achieving your destiny.

Write down four things you will do to free yourself from the condemnation of sin.

1. _____
2. _____
3. _____
4. _____

Meditate on this verse today.

"Therefore there is now no condemnation for those who are in Christ Jesus" (Romans 8:1).

Daily Prayer

Father thank you for the gift of eternal life, may I never take it for granted.

Abiding Day 22

John 10:28
"And I give eternal life to them, and they will never perish; and no one will snatch them out of My hand."

E ternal life: what a promise and a gift we inherit as heirs of salvation through Jesus. As a believer, this is the most precious verse for me to know that I will never perish; my soul has been spared from Hell.

See, friend, the Bible tells us from the book of Romans 6:23, "For the wages of sin is death; but the gift of God is eternal life through Jesus Christ our Lord."

We are born with a sinful nature. Many parents will tell you they don't have to teach their kids to misbehave; it comes naturally. Even as adults, certain habits we pick up were never taught to us by our parents; some we may pick up out of curiosity, others by the peer pressure of society. Regardless, we all have some kind of sin in our lives and are in need of God's mercy.

In the early 2000s, right after graduating college, I worked at a women's shelter in Greenville, SC. It was one of the most rewarding jobs of my life. I had so many opportunities to share God's love with so many women.

One of the most popular words I remember hearing from most of the ladies I had the privilege to come in contact with was "feeling unloved by God and the rest of the world."

You see, most of these women have been physically, sexually, and emotionally abused throughout their lives. Most of them lost hope because of all the pain and suffering they had to endure. Some didn't even know about the love of God.

Once they hear about this precious God who loves them so much and gave Himself as a sacrifice so they may have eternal life, most of them never look back. The love and the gift of God were their only hope.

Write down four ways you will start sharing this precious news with the world.

1. _____
2. _____
3. _____
4. _____

Meditate on this verse today.

"And I give eternal life to them, and they will never perish; and no one will snatch them out of My hand" (John 10:28).

Daily Prayer

Lord teach me how to hide your word in my heart so my heart will not have room for nothing else.

Abiding Day 23

1 John 3:6
"No one who abides in Him sins; no one who sins has
seen Him or knows Him."

W hen we develop a true fellowship and connection with Christ, it is very hard to continue to sin willingly. Once you make the decision to receive Jesus as your Savior, there is some level of spiritual growth that takes place. The level of spiritual growth is based on how much time and effort you put into staying abiding in the Lord.

Growing up, my father taught us to pray every night before we went to bed and before each meal, but I never took the time to read the Word and spend quality time with the Holy Spirit.

After I made the decision to open my heart to Jesus, I started to spend time reading the Word once a week. This lasted for several years. As I grew more mature in the Lord, I felt the urge to spend more quality time with Him. My once-a-week time with the Lord increased to three to four times a week. By the time I got to college, I was spending time with the Lord daily.

As my intimate time with the Lord increases, my sinful nature decreases. I was more sensitive to sin. I was more kind and more loving toward people. The things that used to make me upset now don't matter so much. I was more committed to serving other people.

A couple of years ago, I had a conversation with a friend of mine, who told me how much my friendship had touched her life. I was very intrigued to hear her testimony since she mentioned the Lord had used me to play a part in her journey.

I felt the need to start a prayer group fifteen years prior to her sharing her testimony with me. After much prayer, four of my very good friends decided we would meet every Friday night to pray. The main focus of the prayer was for godly spouses. Every Friday night for one year, the four of us would meet at 8 PM to pray and worship the Lord. What I didn't know at that time was that the Lord was using that prayer group to help sanctify my friend unto the image of Christ. Little by little, as she continues to abide in Christ, her desires for the things of the world become less interesting. Not only did God answer her prayer and bless her with a godly husband, but now she is in full-time ministry, winning souls for the kingdom of God. I truly believe her ministry for the kingdom began the day she made prayer and abiding in the Lord a priority.

We have so much negativity going on in our world today that it is imperative for us to stay focused and abide in the Lord through prayer, fasting, and worship. As you stay abiding in the Lord, you will discover your true calling in the kingdom of God.

List four things you will start incorporating into your daily life to increase your quality time with the Lord.

1. _____

2. _____

3. _____

4. _____

Meditate on this verse today.

"No one who abides in Him sins; no one who sins has seen Him or knows Him" (1 John 3:6).

Daily Prayer

Father help me to increase my daily time with you so I can gain more wisdom and knowledge about your kingdom.

Abiding Day 24

1 John 4:13
"By this we know that we abide in Him and He in us,
because He has given us of His Spirit."

The work of the Holy Spirit in a believer's life is the best way to a successful journey. I mentioned before how my spiritual journey gets stronger as I spend more time with the Lord.

After graduating high school, I had the option to go to college at a university in Maryland, the state I was living in at the time; Chicago, where a very good friend was living; or South Carolina, where my adopted grandparent was living. The difference between the three universities was that the one in South Carolina was a Christian university.

Remember, I mentioned during my early years as a believer that I was spending once a week with the Lord. As little as this time may have been, the Holy Spirit was still faithful to lead me to make the right choice and go to Bob Jones University. So you see, Jesus will meet you where you are in your spiritual journey. The key is to start somewhere.

I cannot say this enough. My Christian maturity intensified during my college years. The school had a policy that no matter what major you decided on, you had to have a Bible course each semester. They had a daily chapel where they had singing and a daily sermon to help students grow in the Lord. They had activities where you could get involved in the community to help others grow in the Lord.

Until my freshman year at Bob Jones University, I had never spent so much time with the Lord. I found myself praying to the Lord about everything I had going in my life. God became my best friend. Every day I look forward to spending time with God.

I have learned the true meaning of 1 Thessalonians when Paul told us to "pray without ceasing" (1 Thessalonians 5:17). I didn't make any decisions without first talking it over with the Lord.

I felt nothing was out of my reach. The Holy Spirit was working so strongly in my life. I was blessed spiritually, emotionally, and physically. My Christian walk was getting stronger every day. By the time I graduated from college, my love for the Lord and others had grown so much. I knew my calling was to serve others and see all souls come to the kingdom of God.

Write down four things you will do daily to be a blessing to others in your community. After all, we are blessed to be a blessing to others.

1. _____
2. _____
3. _____
4. _____

Meditate on this verse today.

"By this we know that we abide in Him and He in us, because He has given us of His Spirit" (1 John 4:13).

Daily Prayer

Father may I keep my eyes focus on heavenly things so I don't get distracted by the things of this world.

Abiding Day 25

John 16:33

"These things I have spoken to you, so that in Me you may have peace. In the world you have tribulation, but take courage; I have overcome the world."

Anyone alive today can attest to all of the trials we are currently experiencing in this world. There is hardship everywhere. Even in the most blessed country in the world, like America, people are going through hard times.

I was born in Haiti at a very young age. My family moved to Maryland, where I grew up. It was such a blessing and privilege to grow up in America. God provides everything for my family: work, shelter, food, a good support system, a wonderful church family, and a great education.

My father would take us back to Haiti during the summer months on several occasions, where we would help in the church ministry and a small medical clinic in a small town in northern Haiti; it was such a blessing to see how the people who had so little were so satisfied in the Lord.

The amount of peace they had was far more than a rich person who had everything in America. Many of the people I spoke with in Haiti would tell me their peace comes from God, not their circumstances.

See, if we don't get our eyes away from the chaos of this world, we will live in constant fear, hopelessness, and discouragement.

Our world has so much negativity going on that all a person has to do these days is turn on the television. The media has enough bad news to last a person a lifetime. It is up to us to make a conscious decision and seek Jesus, who promises to overcome the world.

The problem will come, but we don't need to live in fear. There is always a solution. Nothing lasts forever. Every good or bad thing must come to an end. Therefore, we don't need to let the problems of this life consume us. Rather, we need to keep our eye on Jesus, our Lord and Savior, who promises to perfect every situation that concerns us (Psalm 138:8).

No matter what's going on around you, write down four things you will start implementing daily to keep your peace.

1. _____
2. _____
3. _____
4. _____

Meditate on this verse today.

"These things I have spoken to you, so that in Me you may have peace. In the world you have tribulation, but take courage; I have overcome the world" (John 16:33).

Daily Prayer

Lord help me to prioritized seeking the things of the kingdom first.

Abiding Day 26

Ephesians 5:17
"Wherefore be ye not unwise, but understanding what
the will of the Lord Is."

One of the most beloved people in the Bible was King David. God was so fond of King David that He called him a man after His own heart. David was far from perfect. As a matter of fact, David committed murder when he gave orders to his head general to have one of his best soldiers placed in harm's way with the intention of having him killed after getting that soldier's wife pregnant. As a new Christian, I used to wonder how King David found such favor with the Lord after he committed such horrible sins.

I remember asking myself, "Can I have such favor from the Lord as to be called a woman after His own heart?" I decided to go on a Biblical journey to get my answer. I spent months researching Kind David's life, character, weaknesses, and strengths. During my journey, I discovered Kind David's love for God; he wanted to do everything God's way. Even when kind David messed up, he would quickly ask for forgiveness, repent, and continue his earthly mission. His character was trustworthy. King David knew who was in control of his life, and most importantly, he always ensured everyone else knew the power of God; because of King David's character, God was able to count on him.

One of the most memorable stories about King David's life was when he fought the Philistine giant (Goliath). The full story can be found in the book of 1 Samuel 17. King David was a young teenager, not a trained soldier. However, he had enough faith in the Lord to know that God would fight his battle.

See, King David had a previous encounter with the Lord when He delivered him from other struggles and attacks from the enemy. "The Lord who delivered me from the paw of the lion and from the paw of the bear will deliver me from the hand of this Philistine" (1 Samuel 17:370). King David had enough confidence and trust in the Lord to know God would deliver him out of his troubles, and such faith pleased God.

Another character I noticed while studying King David's life was his love for God. No matter the occasion or situation, King David always finds a way to glorify God. One of the most powerful verses King David wrote is found in the book of Psalm 34:1, "I will bless the Lord at all times, His praise shall continually be in my mouth." Such devotion, love, and faith in the Lord set King David apart from the rest.

As believers, we should strive to have such love and devotion for the Lord as King David did. King David was a true example of someone who prioritized knowing and learning everything about God. Spending time with the Lord was his number one priority. Because of King David's love, faith, and obedience to the Lord, he was called a man after God's own heart.

I believe if we commit to seeking God, meditating on His Word, and increasing our faith to believe in God's promises for our lives, we, too, can be called men and women after God's own heart.

Write down four things you will start implementing to be a man or a woman after God's own heart.

1. _____

2. _____

3. _____

4 _____

Meditate on this verse throughout today.

"Thy word have I hid in mine heart, that I might not sin against thee" (Psalm 119:1).

Daily Prayer

Father help me to be persistent in my daily walk with
you.

Abiding Day 27

Colossians 4:2
"Continue in prayer, and watch in the same with thanksgiving."

A life of prayer for a believer is so essential. If we study the lives of spiritual leaders throughout the centuries, we find that prayer was a priority for all of them. Clearly, prayer was a priority for our Lord Jesus, and since Jesus is our example, we should also make prayer a priority.

In Luke chapter 18, Jesus told His disciples a parable to demonstrate to them the importance of always praying and never giving up.

Jesus was our example on earth of how important prayer is. The disciple noticed that He would wake up early each morning and go and pray. They were so intrigued by it that they asked Jesus to teach them how to pray. Imagine out of everything they saw Jesus do (raising the dead, healing the sick, feeding the hungry, opening the eyes of the blind, walking on water, calming a raging sea, etc.) while walking the earth with Him, and the only thing they asked Him was to teach them how to pray, which tells me there must be something powerful in prayer.

Prayer is our lifeline to our heavenly Father, the maker of all things in the heavens, on earth, and in the sea (Psalm 146:6). He alone possesses the road map of our life. Without daily communication and guidance, it is impossible for anyone to reach their full God-giving destiny. One of the best ways I can explain this is with a comparison to our earthly parents.

Most children communicate daily with their earthly parents for guidance and wisdom. Without that daily connection with their earthly parents, making good decisions would be hard. In the same way, if we don't connect with our heavenly Father regularly, it will be very hard for us to make good decisions in our daily situations.

God is ready to meet with us every day as we would like to come to Him many times. He is never too busy to listen to His children. God gave us a personal invitation in Jeremiah 33:3 "Call to me and I will answer you and show you great and mighty things you do not know."

So if we want heavenly intervention, we must stay connected to Heaven through prayers. Jesus is our perfect role model. As we continue to seek Him through prayer, we will become more like Him. To know that God is on our side is enough to continue with this journey called life until we reach our God-giving destiny.

Write down four habits you will implement to make prayer a priority.

1. _____

2. _____

3. _____

4. _____

Meditate on this verse today.

"Pray without ceasing" (1Thessalonians 5:17).

Daily Prayer

Lord thank you for giving your angels charge to watch over me.

Abiding Day 28

Psalm 119:2
"Blessed are they that keep His Testimonies and that seek Him with the whole hearts."

Throughout the Bible, we read that we will find Him if we seek God with all of our hearts. Because of God's character and faithfulness, He will always fulfill His promises to us, so I believe if people devote time and energy to seeking God with all of their hearts, they will find Him.

To try to illustrate this, I am going to take you back to January 15, 2010, when the Lord reached out to me and granted me a heart to know Him on a deeper level. Our family lost my beloved sister after a three-month battle with lung cancer on that day.

On October 10, 2009, my older sister found out she had stage four small cell carcinoma. She was only 38 years old. To make matters worse, her oncologist broke the news that she had less than six months to live. My entire family was devastated. We weren't ready for such news, and the thought of losing my sister was unimaginable. I had a choice to make. I could choose to be upset at God or trust God's promises from Psalm 23 that He would never leave or forsake me.

"Yea though I walk through the valley of the shadow of death, I will fear no evil, for thou art with me" (Psalm 23:4).

From when we found out my sister had cancer to the time the Lord took her to glory, I consciously decided to seek and trust God. The Holy Spirit started to work in my heart and reminded me that nothing touches our lives without God's permission, and no matter what we go through on earth, God will make a way for us to get through it.

By choosing to seek God in my darkest time, it caused me to have more love and passion for God, and as a result, the Lord gave me the comfort I needed to get through the grieving periods of losing my sister.

The night after we buried my sister, I had a long conversation with God. I truly could not comprehend how my life would be without my sister. That night I went to sleep, and God gave me a dream. I was outside my home in South Carolina. Suddenly, I felt the urge to look up at the sky. As soon as I did, I noticed the most beautiful star. At the center of that star, the sky split open. Then I saw a large table nicely decorated with lots of people seated and ready to have dinner. In the middle of the table, I saw my sister with the most beautiful smile, and the sky closed back up, and I woke up.

I was speechless; I shared the dream with my earthly father, who told me it was the Lord's way of telling me my sister was okay and I need not worry. It has been more than ten years since God gave me that dream, and every time I think of my sister, I remember the dream, and my heart is comforted. I believe if I hadn't chosen to seek the Lord through prayer and fasting during my sister's sickness, I would never have received that confirmation from the Lord.

So we have a choice in life; we can choose to seek God in our time of need, or we can choose to seek the world. Seeking God will lead to answers, peace, and understanding, whereas seeking the world will lead to more confusion, depression, fear, and anxiety. My best advice to anyone going through a hard time is to seek God. He never disappoints.

Write down three things you will start implementing to get to know God on a deeper level.

1. _____

2. _____

3. _____

Meditate on this verse.

"The Lord looked down from heaven upon the children of men, to see if there were any that did understand, and seek God" (Psalm 14:2).

Daily Prayer

Father help me to learn how to turn my worries into prayers.

Abiding Day 29

Psalm 73:26
"My flesh and my heart failed: but God is the strength
of my heart, and my portion forever."

If you asked most people whether life is fair, more than half would say no, and to be honest, life can sometimes be unfair. With all the pain in the world and many life discouragements and setbacks, it's very easy to question God's goodness.

Let's face it, we live in a world run by wicked men who sometimes make decisions that can hurt people, and with that pain comes the famous question, "Why does God allow bad things to happen to good people?" If we take time to analyze this question, we can come to the conclusion that bad things happen in the world because of man's sinful nature.

The earth was given to man to govern it. We read in Genesis 1:26, "And God said, let us make man in our image, after our likeness: and let them have dominion over the fish of the sea, and over the fowl of the air, and over the cattle, and over all the earth." The decision to do good or evil rests with men, and the end result, whether good or bad, is based on man's actions.

We all make decisions every single day, some good, others bad. For instance, a husband can decide to be faithful to his wife or cheat on his wife; if he decides to cheat on his wife and his marriage ends, he can't go around blaming God for his mistake. There are consequences for every action or decision; the results depend on whether you choose God's way of doing things or the world's way of doing things. That is why seeking God's daily before making any major decision is so important.

God is our strength; it's important to seek Him in every decision of our lives. We live in a time where pain and suffering are increasing. It is so refreshing to know we have a blessed hope through our Lord and Savior, Jesus Christ.

Write down three things you will do before making any major decision in your life moving forward.

1. _____

2. _____

3. _____

Meditated on this verse

Psalm 23:6 "Surely goodness and mercy shall follow me all the days of my Life: an I will dwell in the house of the Lord forever.

Daily Prayer

Father help me not to ever let worry or fear control my life, rather help me to run to you my shield, my glory the one who lifts my head.

Abiding Day 30

Deuteronomy 31:8

"And the Lord, He it is that doth go before thee; He will be with thee, he will not fail thee, neither forsake thee, fear not, neither be dismayed."

This verse was a promise from God to the children of Israel, and I strongly believe this promise is equally true for Christians today. The Lord will go before us just like He did for the nation of Israel.

One year into my marriage, my husband and I felt strongly about starting a clinic in Haiti; we had no resources or money. We dedicate time to prayer and fasting specifically for wisdom and understanding; the more we seek God, the more real the vision becomes. A year after we started praying and fasting, God opened the door for us to start our first clinic in Haiti. Holy Grace Medical Center wouldn't be here today if we didn't seek God for strength and guidance. The steps to opening the clinic weren't easy. However, we trust God every step of the way because He made a promise to go before us.

Another event in my life that reminded me of how the Lord always goes before me was the time when my college roommate's family made room in their home to accommodate me. In spring 1999, I was getting ready to wrap up my second semester as a freshman at Bob Jones

University. Another for me to return back to school that next semester; I needed $5,000 for my tuition, and I needed to find a job and a place to live close to campus. I remember my sweet roommate asked her parents to help me. Not only did they open their home for me to stay in, but her father arranged for me to have a job, and because of their love towards me, I was able to raise the money that summer and return to school.

Many Christians have faith in God for something; some for healing, others for financial security, and still others for marriage or children. Trust in God to go before you in whatever you believe.

"I will go before thee, and make the crooked places straight" (Isaiah 45:2). For us to experience God's miracles, we must increase our faith to believe that He will do what He promised.

Write down three hindrances in your life that decrease your faith in God.
1. _____
2. _____
3. _____

Write down three ways you will overcome these three hindrances.
1. _____
2. _____
3. _____

Meditate on this verse

Psalms 18: 32 "It is God that girdeth me with strength and maketh my way perfect"

Daily Prayer

Father engrave your word into my mind and spirit that I might not sins against you.

Conclusion

One of the best illustrations of abiding is from the book of John, the 15th chapter. The Lord Jesus gave us an example about the vine and the branches. The Lord explained that the only way a branch can bear fruit is to abide in the vine. Similarly, the only way for us, God's children, to bear fruit is to stay abiding in Jesus.

Picture Jesus as the vine, while we are the branches. If we disconnect ourselves from the Lord, we will most likely encounter problems and troubles. It's hard to be successful without a daily connection with the Lord, and the best way to accomplish that connection is through daily prayer.

In my life here on Earth one thing I have learned is that no one wants to fail. Everyone would like to achieve their best life before leaving this world. Unfortunately, not everyone will get to accomplish that.

The good news is that our heavenly Father gave us His Holy Spirit as a gift to guide us into all truth. Therefore, may we make abiding with Jesus a daily priority so we don't miss our calling before our time is up.

May the Lord bless every person who is reading this devotional book, may you find your purpose in this world.

Daily Prayer

Father may I achieve my purpose at the end of my Life. In Jesus name. Amen.

About the Author

Nanncie Constantin is an acute care nurse practitioner with 18 years of experience in the medical field. She worked in ICU for over 12 years as a nurse, and over 6 years as a nurse practitioner an Emergency medicine and inpatient hospitalist. She is a devoted follower of Jesus Christ for 29 years. Nanncie is a powerful force in the kingdom of God; together with her husband Dr. Osias they started a medical clinic in Haiti where they are changing lives of many wonderful people not only medically but also spiritually. She is a powerful prayer warrior with many personal testimonies on how prayer and a personal relationship with Jesus change her life. Jesus is truly the lover of her soul.